This Book Belongs To

Easy Planners And Journals

To help you organize your life

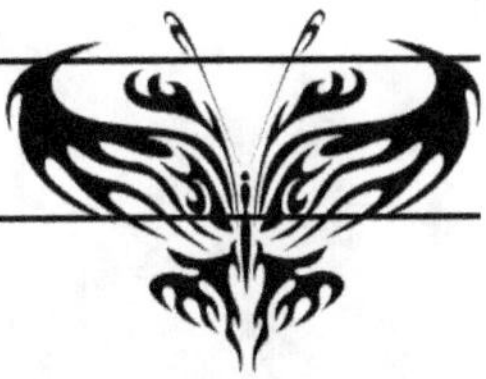

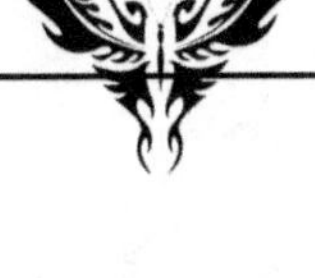

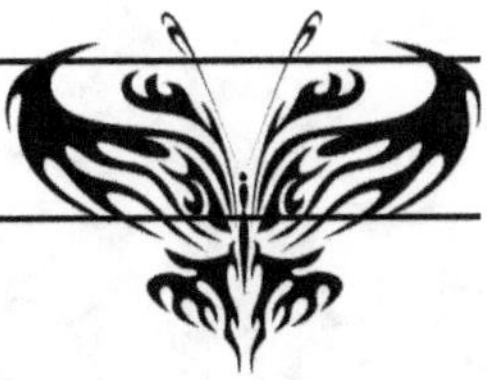

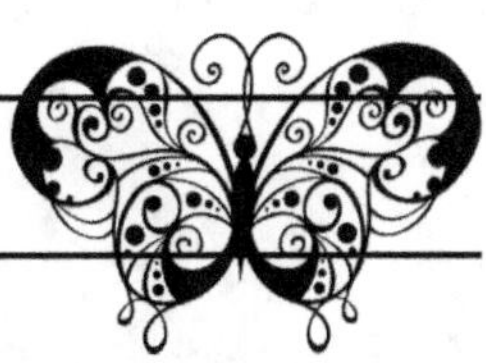

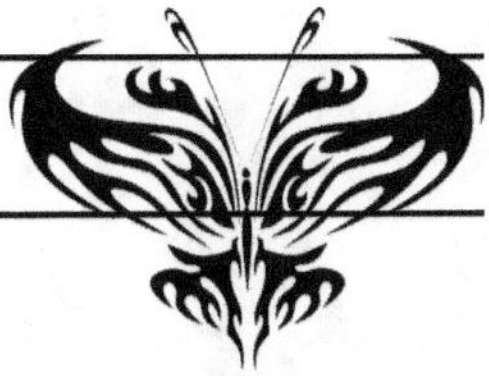

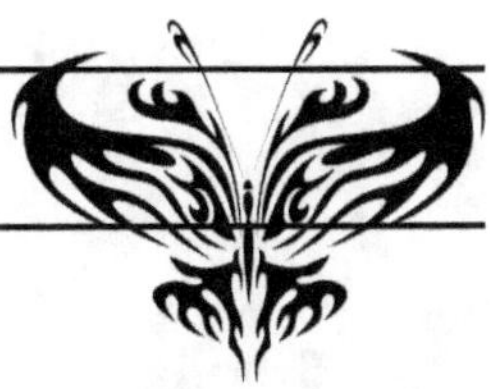

www.ingramcontent.com/pod-product-compliance
Lightning Source LLC
Chambersburg PA
CBHW072050280526
45788CB00006B/2252
* 9 7 8 1 0 9 1 3 2 5 3 5 7 *